A Gift For:

From:

Date:

The Power of God's Word for Fathers
© 2013 by Jack Countryman

Published in Nashville, Tennessee, by Thomas Nelson. Thomas Nelson is a registered trademark of Thomas Nelson, Inc.

Thomas Nelson, Inc., titles may be purchased in bulk for educational, business, fund-raising, or sales promotional use. For information, please e-mail SpecialMarkets@ThomasNelson.com.

Scripture quotations are taken from THE NEW KING JAMES VERSION. © 1982 by Thomas Nelson, Inc. Used by permission. All rights reserved.

ISBN-13: 978-1-4003-2228-2 (with display)
ISBN-13: 978-1-4003-2229-9 (without display)

Printed in the United States of America

13 14 15 16 17 PP 6 5 4 3 2 1

THE
POWER
OF

GOD'S
WORD

FOR
FATHERS

Jack Countryman

A Division of Thomas Nelson Publishers

THOMAS NELSON
Since 1798

NASHVILLE DALLAS MEXICO CITY RIO DE JANEIRO

CONTENTS

GOD'S SPECIAL LOVE IS WITH FATHERS
WHEN . . .

GOD'S
PLAN
FOR

FATHERS

IS . . .

TO WORSHIP GOD

"God is Spirit, and those who worship Him must worship in spirit and truth."

JOHN 4:24

Give to the LORD the glory due His name;
   Bring an offering, and come into His
      courts.
Oh, worship the LORD in the beauty of
      holiness!
   Tremble before Him, all the earth.

PSALM 96:8–9

Exalt the LORD our God,
   And worship at His footstool—
      He is holy. . . .
Exalt the LORD our God,
   And worship at His holy hill;
   For the LORD our God is holy.

PSALM 99:5, 9

For the LORD is the great God,
    And the great King above all gods.
In His hand are the deep places of the earth;
    The heights of the hills are His also.
The sea is His, for He made it;
    And His hands formed the dry land.
Oh come, let us worship and bow down;
    Let us kneel before the LORD our Maker.
For He is our God,
    And we are the people of His pasture,
    And the sheep of His hand.

PSALM 95:3–7

Fear God and give glory to Him, for the hour of His judgment has come; and worship Him who made heaven and earth, the sea and springs of water.

REVELATION 14:7

TO OBEY GOD'S WORD

For the word of God is living and powerful, and sharper than any two-edged sword, piercing even to the division of soul and spirit, and of joints and marrow, and is a discerner of the thoughts and intents of the heart.

HEBREWS 4:12

The law of the LORD is perfect, converting the
        soul;
    The testimony of the LORD is sure,
        making wise the simple;
The statutes of the LORD are right, rejoicing
        the heart;
    The commandment of the LORD is pure,
        enlightening the eyes.

PSALM 19:7–8

Draw near to God and He will draw near to you. Cleanse your hands, you sinners; and purify your hearts, you double-minded.

JAMES 4:8

As for God, His way is perfect;
The word of the LORD is proven;
He is a shield to all who trust in Him.

PSALM 18:30

For whatever things were written before were written for our learning, that we through the patience and comfort of the Scriptures might have hope.

ROMANS 15:4

TO COME TO GOD IN PRAYER

"Ask, and it will be given to you; seek, and you will find; knock, and it will be opened to you. For everyone who asks receives, and he who seeks finds, and to him who knocks it will be opened."

MATTHEW 7:7–8

Be anxious for nothing, but in everything by prayer and supplication, with thanksgiving, let your requests be made known to God; and the peace of God, which surpasses all understanding, will guard your hearts and minds through Christ Jesus.

PHILIPPIANS 4:6–7

Rejoice always, pray without ceasing, in everything give thanks; for this is the will of God in Christ Jesus for you.

1 THESSALONIANS 5:16–18

Hear me when I call, O God of my
        righteousness!
    You have relieved me in my distress;
    Have mercy on me, and hear my prayer.

PSALM 4:1

TO LISTEN TO THE HOLY SPIRIT

But those who wait on the LORD
>   Shall renew their strength;
>   They shall mount up with wings like
>   eagles,
>   They shall run and not be weary,
>   They shall walk and not faint.

ISAIAH 40:31

"For everyone who asks receives, and he who seeks finds, and to him who knocks it will be opened. If a son asks for bread from any father among you, will he give him a stone? Or if he asks for a fish, will he give him a serpent instead of a fish? Or if he asks for an egg, will he offer him a scorpion? If you then, being evil, know how to give good gifts to your children, how much more will your heavenly Father give the Holy Spirit to those who ask Him!"

LUKE 11:10–13

"If you ask anything in My name, I will do it.

"If you love Me, keep My commandments. And I will pray the Father, and He will give you another Helper, that He may abide with you forever—the Spirit of truth, whom the world cannot receive, because it neither sees Him nor knows Him; but you know Him, for He dwells with you and will be in you. I will not leave you orphans; I will come to you. . . .

"But the Helper, the Holy Spirit, whom the Father will send in My name, He will teach you all things, and bring to your remembrance all things that I said to you."

JOHN 14:14–18, 26

GOD
FREELY
GIVES TO

FATHERS . . .

ETERNAL HOPE
FOR LIFE

But let us who are of the day be sober, putting on the breastplate of faith and love, and as a helmet the hope of salvation. For God did not appoint us to wrath, but to obtain salvation through our Lord Jesus Christ, who died for us, that whether we wake or sleep, we should live together with Him.

Therefore comfort each other and edify one another, just as you also are doing.

1 THESSALONIANS 5:8–11

Blessed be the God and Father of our Lord Jesus Christ, who according to His abundant mercy has begotten us again to a living hope through the resurrection of Jesus Christ from the dead, to an inheritance incorruptible and undefiled and that does not fade away, reserved in heaven for you, who are kept by the power of God through faith for salvation ready to be revealed in the last time.

1 PETER 1:3–5

For as many as are led by the Spirit of God, these are sons of God. For you did not receive the spirit of bondage again to fear, but you received the Spirit of adoption by whom we cry out, "Abba, Father." The Spirit Himself bears witness with our spirit that we are children of God, and if children, then heirs—heirs of God and joint heirs with Christ, if indeed we suffer with Him, that we may also be glorified together.

For I consider that the sufferings of this present time are not worthy to be compared with the glory which shall be revealed in us. . . . For we were saved in this hope, but hope that is seen is not hope; for why does one still hope for what he sees? But if we hope for what we do not see, we eagerly wait for it with perseverance.

ROMANS 8:14–18, 24–25

We give thanks to the God and Father of our Lord Jesus Christ. . . . Because of the hope which is laid up for you in heaven . . . which has come to you, as it has also in all the world, and is bringing forth fruit, as it is also among you since the day you heard and knew the grace of God in truth.

COLOSSIANS 1:3, 5–6

WISDOM FOR EACH DAY

My son, pay attention to my wisdom;
Lend your ear to my understanding,
That you may preserve discretion,
And your lips may keep knowledge.

PROVERBS 5:1–2

The fear of the LORD is the beginning of
wisdom;
A good understanding have all those
who do His commandments.
His praise endures forever.

PSALM 111:10

If any of you lacks wisdom, let him ask of
God, who gives to all liberally and without
reproach, and it will be given to him. But let
him ask in faith, with no doubting, for he who
doubts is like a wave of the sea driven and
tossed by the wind.

JAMES 1:5–6

"Get wisdom! Get understanding!
>   Do not forget, nor turn away from the
>   words of my mouth.
Do not forsake her, and she will preserve you;
>   Love her, and she will keep you.
Wisdom is the principal thing;
>   Therefore get wisdom.
>   And in all your getting, get
>   understanding.
Exalt her, and she will promote you;
>   She will bring you honor, when you
>   embrace her.
She will place on your head an ornament of
>   grace;
>   A crown of glory she will deliver to you."
Hear, my son, and receive my sayings,
>   And the years of your life will be many.
I have taught you in the way of wisdom;
>   I have led you in right paths.

PROVERBS 4:5–11

How much better to get wisdom than gold!
>   And to get understanding is to be chosen
>   rather than silver.

PROVERBS 16:16

VICTORY OVER SIN

Therefore, if anyone is in Christ, he is a new creation; old things have passed away; behold, all things have become new. Now all things are of God, who has reconciled us to Himself through Jesus Christ, and has given us the ministry of reconciliation, that is, that God was in Christ reconciling the world to Himself, not imputing their trespasses to them, and has committed to us the word of reconciliation.

Now then, we are ambassadors for Christ, as though God were pleading through us: we implore you on Christ's behalf, be reconciled to God. For He made Him who knew no sin to be sin for us, that we might become the righteousness of God in Him.

2 Corinthians 5:17–21

This is the message which we have heard from Him and declare to you, that God is light and in Him is no darkness at all. If we say that we have fellowship with Him, and walk in darkness, we lie and do not practice the truth. But if we walk in the light as He is in the light, we have fellowship with one another, and the blood of Jesus Christ His Son cleanses us from all sin.

If we say that we have no sin, we deceive ourselves, and the truth is not in us. If we confess our sins, He is faithful and just to forgive us our sins and to cleanse us from all unrighteousness. If we say that we have not sinned, we make Him a liar, and His word is not in us.

1 JOHN 1:5–10

And you know that He was manifested to take away our sins, and in Him there is no sin. Whoever abides in Him does not sin. Whoever sins has neither seen Him nor known Him. . . .

Let no one deceive you. He who practices righteousness is righteous, just as He is righteous.

1 JOHN 3:5–7

"Wash yourselves, make yourselves clean;
    Put away the evil of your doings from
        before My eyes.
    Cease to do evil,
Learn to do good;
    Seek justice,
    Rebuke the oppressor;
    Defend the fatherless,
    Plead for the widow.
"Come now, and let us reason together. . . .
    Though your sins are like scarlet,
    They shall be as white as snow;
    Though they are red like crimson,
    They shall be as wool.
If you are willing and obedient,
    You shall eat the good of the land."

Isaiah 1:16–19

PEACE IN
TROUBLED TIMES

I will bless the Lord at all times;
>   His praise shall continually be in my
>   mouth.
My soul shall make its boast in the Lord;
>   The humble shall hear of it and be glad.
Oh, magnify the Lord with me,
>   And let us exalt His name together.
I sought the Lord, and He heard me,
>   And delivered me from all my fears.
They looked to Him and were radiant,
>   And their faces were not ashamed.
This poor man cried out, and the Lord
>   heard him,
>   And saved him out of all his troubles.
The angel of the Lord encamps all around
>   those who fear Him,
>   And delivers them.
Oh, taste and see that the Lord is good;
>   Blessed is the man who trusts in Him!

PSALM 34:1–8

"Peace I leave with you, My peace I give to you; not as the world gives do I give to you. Let not your heart be troubled, neither let it be afraid."

JOHN 14:27

Trust in the LORD with all your heart,
    And lean not on your own
        understanding;
In all your ways acknowledge Him,
    And He shall direct your paths.

PROVERBS 3:5–6

[Cast] all your care upon Him, for He cares for you.

Be sober, be vigilant; because your adversary the devil walks about like a roaring lion, seeking whom he may devour. Resist him, steadfast in the faith, knowing that the same sufferings are experienced by your brotherhood in the world. But may the God of all grace, who called us to His eternal glory by Christ Jesus, after you have suffered a while, perfect, establish, strengthen, and settle you. To Him be the glory and the dominion forever and ever. Amen.

1 PETER 5:7–11

POWER TO DEFEAT THEIR DEEPEST FEARS

I will love You, O Lord, my strength.
The Lord is my rock and my fortress and
        my deliverer;
    My God, my strength, in whom I will
        trust;
    My shield and the horn of my salvation,
        my stronghold.
I will call upon the Lord, who is worthy to
        be praised;
    So shall I be saved from my enemies.

PSALM 18:1–3

"I am the light of the world. He who follows Me shall not walk in darkness, but have the light of life."

JOHN 8:12

The Lord is my light and my salvation;
 Whom shall I fear?
 The Lord is the strength of my life;
 Of whom shall I be afraid? . . .
My enemies and foes,
 They stumbled and fell.
Though an army may encamp against me,
 My heart shall not fear;
 Though war may rise against me,
 In this I will be confident.
One thing I have desired of the Lord,
 That will I seek:
 That I may dwell in the house of the Lord
 All the days of my life,
 To behold the beauty of the Lord,
 And to inquire in His temple.
For in the time of trouble
 He shall hide me in His pavilion;
 In the secret place of His tabernacle
 He shall hide me;
 He shall set me high upon a rock.

PSALM 27:1–5

COURAGE TO BE MEN OF INTEGRITY

Dishonest scales are an abomination to the
LORD,
But a just weight is His delight.
When pride comes, then comes shame;
But with the humble is wisdom.
The integrity of the upright will guide them,
But the perversity of the unfaithful will
destroy them.

PROVERBS 11:1–3

The righteous man walks in his integrity;
His children are blessed after him.

PROVERBS 20:7

The LORD shall judge the peoples;
Judge me, O LORD, according to my
righteousness,
And according to my integrity within
me.

PSALM 7:8

Blessed is the man
> Who walks not in the counsel of the
> > ungodly,
> > Nor stands in the path of sinners,
> > Nor sits in the seat of the scornful;

But his delight is in the law of the Lord,
> And in His law he meditates day and
> > night.

He shall be like a tree
> Planted by the rivers of water,
> That brings forth its fruit in its season,
> Whose leaf also shall not wither;
> And whatever he does shall prosper.

The ungodly are not so,
> But are like the chaff which the wind
> > drives away.

Therefore the ungodly shall not stand in the
> > judgment,
> Nor sinners in the congregation of the
> > righteous.

For the Lord knows the way of the righteous,
> But the way of the ungodly shall perish.

Psalm 1:1–6

GOD
ASKS

FATHERS

TO . . .

WITNESS TO THE LOST

"Behold, I stand at the door and knock. If anyone hears My voice and opens the door, I will come in to him and dine with him, and he with Me."

REVELATION 3:20

"Go therefore and make disciples of all the nations, baptizing them in the name of the Father and of the Son and of the Holy Spirit, teaching them to observe all things that I have commanded you; and lo, I am with you always, even to the end of the age." Amen.

MATTHEW 28:19–20

"Whoever confesses Me before men, him the Son of Man also will confess before the angels of God. But he who denies Me before men will be denied before the angels of God."

LUKE 12:8–9

Therefore God also has highly exalted Him and given Him the name which is above every name, that at the name of Jesus every knee should bow, of those in heaven, and of those on earth, and of those under the earth, and that every tongue should confess that Jesus Christ is Lord, to the glory of God the Father.

PHILIPPIANS 2:9–11

"Let your light so shine before men, that they may see your good works and glorify your Father in heaven."

MATTHEW 5:16

LOVE THEIR NEIGHBORS

"You shall love your neighbor as yourself."

MATTHEW 19:19

"You shall not bear false witness against your neighbor.

"You shall not covet your neighbor's house; you shall not covet your neighbor's wife, nor his male servant, nor his female servant, nor his ox, nor his donkey, nor anything that is your neighbor's."

EXODUS 20:16–17

Do not say to your neighbor,
     "Go, and come back,
        And tomorrow I will give it,"
        When you have it with you.
Do not devise evil against your neighbor,
        For he dwells by you for safety's sake.

PROVERBS 3:28–29

He who despises his neighbor sins;
But he who has mercy on the poor, happy
is he.

PROVERBS 14:21

He who is devoid of wisdom despises his
neighbor,
But a man of understanding holds his
peace.

PROVERBS 11:12

INSTRUCT THEIR CHILDREN IN THE WORD

Hear, my children, the instruction of a father,
    And give attention to know
        understanding;
For I give you good doctrine:
    Do not forsake my law.
When I was my father's son,
    Tender and the only one in the sight of
        my mother,
He also taught me, and said to me:
    "Let your heart retain my words;
    Keep my commands, and live. . . ."
My son, give attention to my words;
    Incline your ear to my sayings.
Do not let them depart from your eyes;
    Keep them in the midst of your heart;
For they are life to those who find them,
    And health to all their flesh.

PROVERBS 4:1–4, 20–22

Now therefore, listen to me, my children,
For blessed are those who keep my ways.
Hear instruction and be wise,
And do not disdain it.
Blessed is the man who listens to me,
Watching daily at my gates,
Waiting at the posts of my doors.
For whoever finds me finds life,
And obtains favor from the Lord.

PROVERBS 8:32–35

A wise man will hear and increase learning,
And a man of understanding will attain
wise counsel,
To understand a proverb and an enigma,
The words of the wise and their riddles.
The fear of the Lord is the beginning of
knowledge,
But fools despise wisdom and instruction.
My son, hear the instruction of your father,
And do not forsake the law of your
mother;
For they will be a graceful ornament on
your head,
And chains about your neck.

PROVERBS 1:5–9

TEACH THEIR CHILDREN TO PRAY

Let us therefore come boldly to the throne of grace, that we may obtain mercy and find grace to help in time of need.

HEBREWS 4:16

"Call to Me, and I will answer you, and show you great and mighty things, which you do not know."

JEREMIAH 33:3

Be anxious for nothing, but in everything by prayer and supplication, with thanksgiving, let your requests be made known to God; and the peace of God, which surpasses all understanding, will guard your hearts and minds through Christ Jesus.

PHILIPPIANS 4:6–7

Likewise the Spirit also helps in our weaknesses. For we do not know what we should pray for as we ought, but the Spirit Himself makes intercession for us with groanings which cannot be uttered. Now He who searches the hearts knows what the mind of the Spirit is, because He makes intercession for the saints according to the will of God.

And we know that all things work together for good to those who love God, to those who are the called according to His purpose.

ROMANS 8:26–28

"Therefore I say to you, whatever things you ask when you pray, believe that you receive them, and you will have them."

MARK 11:24

GOD ASKS FATHERS TO...
TRUST GOD

Trust in the LORD with all your heart,
    And lean not on your own
        understanding;
In all your ways acknowledge Him,
    And He shall direct your paths.

PROVERBS 3:5–6

And he said:
    "The LORD is my rock and my fortress
        and my deliverer;
The God of my strength, in whom I will trust;
    My shield and the horn of my salvation,
    My stronghold and my refuge;
    My Savior, You save me from violence."

2 SAMUEL 22:2–3

Preserve me, O God, for in You I put my trust.
O my soul, you have said to the LORD,
    "You are my LORD,
    My goodness is nothing apart from You."

PSALM 16:1–2

But know that the LORD has set apart for
    Himself him who is godly;
  The LORD will hear when I call to Him.
Be angry, and do not sin.
    Meditate within your heart on your bed,
      and be still. *Selah*.
Offer the sacrifices of righteousness,
    And put your trust in the LORD.

PSALM 4:3–5

In the day of my trouble I will call upon You,
    For You will answer me.
Among the gods there is none like You,
    O Lord;
    Nor are there any works like Your works.
All nations whom You have made
    Shall come and worship before You,
    O LORD,
    And shall glorify Your name.
For You are great, and do wondrous things;
    You alone are God.

PSALM 86:7–10

TEACH THEIR CHILDREN GRATITUDE

Let your conduct be without covetousness; be content with such things as you have. For He Himself has said, "I will never leave you nor forsake you."

HEBREWS 13:5

Sing praise to the LORD, you saints of His,
    And give thanks at the remembrance of
        His holy name.
For His anger is but for a moment,
    His favor is for life;
    Weeping may endure for a night,
    But joy comes in the morning.
Now in my prosperity I said,
    "I shall never be moved."

PSALM 30:4–6

Finally, brethren, whatever things are true, whatever things are noble, whatever things are just, whatever things are pure, whatever things are lovely, whatever things are of good report, if there is any virtue and if there is anything praiseworthy—meditate on these things. The things which you learned and received and heard and saw in me, these do, and the God of peace will be with you.

But I rejoiced in the Lord greatly that now at last your care for me has flourished again; though you surely did care, but you lacked opportunity. Not that I speak in regard to need, for I have learned in whatever state I am, to be content.

Philippians 4:8–11

Make a joyful shout to the Lord, all you lands!
  Serve the Lord with gladness;
  Come before His presence with singing.

Psalm 100:1–2

SHOW KINDNESS TO THEIR FAMILIES

Let all bitterness, wrath, anger, clamor, and evil speaking be put away from you, with all malice. And be kind to one another, tender-hearted, forgiving one another, even as God in Christ forgave you.

EPHESIANS 4:31–32

You are witnesses, and God also, how devoutly and justly and blamelessly we behaved ourselves among you who believe; as you know how we exhorted, and comforted, and charged every one of you, as a father does his own children, that you would walk worthy of God who calls you into His own kingdom and glory.

1 THESSALONIANS 2:10–12

Hatred stirs up strife,
But love covers all sins.

PROVERBS 10:12

"Or what man is there among you who, if his son asks for bread, will give him a stone? . . . If you then, being evil, know how to give good gifts to your children, how much more will your Father who is in heaven give good things to those who ask Him!"

MATTHEW 7:9, 11

GOD
GIVES

FATHERS

STRENGTH
WHEN . . .

THEY COMFORT THEIR LOVED ONES

"Fear not, for I am with you;
> Be not dismayed, for I am your God.
> I will strengthen you,
> Yes, I will help you,
> I will uphold you with My righteous right
> hand. . . .

"Behold, I will make you into a new threshing
> sledge with sharp teeth;
> You shall thresh the mountains and beat
> them small,
> And make the hills like chaff.

You shall winnow them, the wind shall carry
> them away,
> And the whirlwind shall scatter them;
> You shall rejoice in the Lord,
> And glory in the Holy One of Israel."

ISAIAH 41:10, 15–16

"Not one [sparrow] falls to the ground apart from your Father's will. But the very hairs of your head are all numbered. Do not fear therefore; you are of more value than many sparrows."

MATTHEW 10:29–31

But the mercy of the LORD is from everlasting
        to everlasting
    On those who fear Him,
    And His righteousness to children's
        children.

PSALM 103:17

Blessed be the God and Father of our Lord Jesus Christ, the Father of mercies and God of all comfort, who comforts us in all our tribulation, that we may be able to comfort those who are in any trouble, with the comfort with which we ourselves are comforted by God. For as the sufferings of Christ abound in us, so our consolation also abounds through Christ.

2 CORINTHIANS 1:3–5

LOVED ONES DIE

But I do not want you to be ignorant, brethren, concerning those who have fallen asleep, lest you sorrow as others who have no hope. For if we believe that Jesus died and rose again, even so God will bring with Him those who sleep in Jesus.

For this we say to you by the word of the Lord, that we who are alive and remain until the coming of the Lord will by no means precede those who are asleep. For the Lord Himself will descend from heaven with a shout, with the voice of an archangel, and with the trumpet of God. And the dead in Christ will rise first.

1 THESSALONIANS 4:13–16

He heals the brokenhearted
    And binds up their wounds.
He counts the number of the stars;
    He calls them all by name.
Great is our Lord, and mighty in power;
    His understanding is infinite.

PSALM 147:3–5

For I am persuaded that neither death nor life, nor angels nor principalities nor powers, nor things present nor things to come, nor height nor depth, nor any other created thing, shall be able to separate us from the love of God which is in Christ Jesus our Lord.

ROMANS 8:38–39

THEY ARE ANGRY
AND NEED PEACE

So then, my beloved brethren, let every man be swift to hear, slow to speak, slow to wrath; for the wrath of man does not produce the righteousness of God.

JAMES 1:19–20

He who is slow to anger is better than the
mighty,
And he who rules his spirit than he who
takes a city.

PROVERBS 16:32

Let your speech always be with grace, seasoned with salt, that you may know how you ought to answer each one.

COLOSSIANS 4:6

"Be angry, and do not sin": do not let the sun go down on your wrath.

EPHESIANS 4:26

Now I plead with you, brethren, by the name of our Lord Jesus Christ, that you all speak the same thing, and that there be no divisions among you, but that you be perfectly joined together in the same mind and in the same judgment.

1 CORINTHIANS 1:10

THEIR CHILDREN DISOBEY THEM

Children, obey your parents in the Lord, for this is right. . . . And you, fathers, do not provoke your children to wrath, but bring them up in the training and admonition of the Lord.

EPHESIANS 6:1, 4

"If his sons forsake My law
    And do not walk in My judgments,
If they break My statutes
    And do not keep My commandments,
Then I will punish their transgression with
        the rod,
    And their iniquity with stripes.
Nevertheless My lovingkindness I will not
        utterly take from him,
    Nor allow My faithfulness to fail.
My covenant I will not break,
    Nor alter the word that has gone out of
        My lips."

PSALM 89:30–34

48

Foolishness is bound up in the heart of a
    child;
        The rod of correction will drive it far
        from him.

PROVERBS 22:15

A wise son heeds his father's instruction,
    But a scoffer does not listen to rebuke.

PROVERBS 13:1

As a father pities his children,
    So the LORD pities those who fear Him.
For He knows our frame;
    He remembers that we are dust.
As for man, his days are like grass;
    As a flower of the field, so he flourishes.
For the wind passes over it, and it is gone,
    And its place remembers it no more.
But the mercy of the LORD is from everlasting
        to everlasting
    On those who fear Him,
    And His righteousness to children's
    children.

PSALM 103:13–17

THEIR FAMILIES GROW APART

A merry heart makes a cheerful countenance,
> But by sorrow of the heart the spirit is
> broken.
The heart of him who has understanding
> seeks knowledge,
> But the mouth of fools feeds on
> foolishness.
All the days of the afflicted are evil,
> But he who is of a merry heart has a
> continual feast.
Better is a little with the fear of the LORD,
> Than great treasure with trouble.

PROVERBS 15:13–16

God sets the solitary in families;
> He brings out those who are bound into
> prosperity;
> But the rebellious dwell in a dry land.

PSALM 68:6

Therefore my spirit is overwhelmed within
me;
My heart within me is distressed.
I remember the days of old;
I meditate on all Your works;
I muse on the work of Your hands.
I spread out my hands to You;
My soul longs for You like a thirsty land.
Selah.
Answer me speedily, O Lord;
My spirit fails!
Do not hide Your face from me,
Lest I be like those who go down into
the pit.
Cause me to hear Your lovingkindness in the
morning,
For in You do I trust;
Cause me to know the way in which I
should walk,
For I lift up my soul to You.

PSALM 143:4–8

GOD
CHALLENGES

FATHERS

TO . . .

GROW IN THEIR CHRISTIAN WALKS

Teach me, O Lord, the way of Your statutes,
   And I shall keep it to the end.
Give me understanding, and I shall keep
      Your law;
      Indeed, I shall observe it with my whole
      heart.
Make me walk in the path of Your
      commandments,
   For I delight in it.

PSALM 119:33–35

Now by this we know that we know Him, if we keep His commandments. He who says, "I know Him," and does not keep His commandments, is a liar, and the truth is not in him. But whoever keeps His word, truly the love of God is perfected in him. By this we know that we are in Him. He who says he abides in Him ought himself also to walk just as He walked.

1 JOHN 2:3–6

Teach me Your way, O Lord;
  I will walk in Your truth;
  Unite my heart to fear Your name.
I will praise You, O Lord my God, with all
      my heart,
  And I will glorify Your name
      forevermore.

PSALM 86:11–12

Your word is a lamp to my feet
  And a light to my path.
I have sworn and confirmed
  That I will keep Your righteous
      judgments.
I am afflicted very much;
  Revive me, O Lord, according to Your
      word.
Accept, I pray, the freewill offerings of my
      mouth, O Lord,
  And teach me Your judgments.
My life is continually in my hand,
  Yet I do not forget Your law.

PSALM 119:105–109

DEAL HONESTLY WITH OTHERS

"Judge not, that you be not judged. For with what judgment you judge, you will be judged; and with the measure you use, it will be measured back to you. And why do you look at the speck in your brother's eye, but do not consider the plank in your own eye? . . . Hypocrite! First remove the plank from your own eye, and then you will see clearly to remove the speck from your brother's eye."

MATTHEW 7:1–3, 5

If indeed you have heard Him and have been taught by Him, as the truth is in Jesus: that you put off, concerning your former conduct, the old man which grows corrupt according to the deceitful lusts, and be renewed in the spirit of your mind.

EPHESIANS 4:21–23

Do not withhold good from those to whom it
      is due,
    When it is in the power of your hand to
      do so.

PROVERBS 3:27

Do not lie to one another, since you have put
off the old man with his deeds, and have put
on the new man who is renewed in knowledge
according to the image of Him who created
him.

COLOSSIANS 3:9–10

Lying lips are an abomination to the LORD,
    But those who deal truthfully are His
      delight.

PROVERBS 12:22

ASK FORGIVENESS OF OTHERS

"Take heed to yourselves. If your brother sins against you, rebuke him; and if he repents, forgive him. And if he sins against you seven times in a day, and seven times in a day returns to you, saying, 'I repent,' you shall forgive him."

LUKE 17:3–4

The wicked flee when no one pursues,
    But the righteous are bold as a lion.
Because of the transgression of a land, many
        are its princes;
    But by a man of understanding and
        knowledge
    Right will be prolonged.
A poor man who oppresses the poor
    Is like a driving rain which leaves no
        food.

PROVERBS 28:1–3

"And whenever you stand praying, if you have anything against anyone, forgive him, that your Father in heaven may also forgive you your trespasses. But if you do not forgive, neither will your Father in heaven forgive your trespasses."

MARK 11:25–26

I, therefore, the prisoner of the Lord, beseech you to walk worthy of the calling with which you were called, with all lowliness and gentleness, with longsuffering, bearing with one another in love, endeavoring to keep the unity of the Spirit in the bond of peace.

EPHESIANS 4:1–3

Repay no one evil for evil. Have regard for good things in the sight of all men. If it is possible, as much as depends on you, live peaceably with all men. Beloved, do not avenge yourselves, but rather give place to wrath; for it is written, "Vengeance is Mine, I will repay," says the Lord.

ROMANS 12:17–19

SHARE THEIR FAITH WITH OTHERS

Brethren, if anyone among you wanders from the truth, and someone turns him back, let him know that he who turns a sinner from the error of his way will save a soul from death and cover a multitude of sins.

JAMES 5:19–20

But what does it say? "The word is near you, in your mouth and in your heart" (that is, the word of faith which we preach): that if you confess with your mouth the Lord Jesus and believe in your heart that God has raised Him from the dead, you will be saved. For with the heart one believes unto righteousness, and with the mouth confession is made unto salvation. For the Scripture says, "Whoever believes on Him will not be put to shame."

ROMANS 10:8–11

"Most assuredly, I say to you, he who believes in Me, the works that I do he will do also; and greater works than these he will do, because I go to My Father. And whatever you ask in My name, that I will do, that the Father may be glorified in the Son."

JOHN 14:12–13

And let us not grow weary while doing good, for in due season we shall reap if we do not lose heart. Therefore, as we have opportunity, let us do good to all, especially to those who are of the household of faith.

GALATIANS 6:9–10

"Give, and it will be given to you: good measure, pressed down, shaken together, and running over will be put into your bosom. For with the same measure that you use, it will be measured back to you."

LUKE 6:38

BE WISE WITH THEIR FINANCES

Now it shall come to pass, if you diligently obey the voice of the LORD your God, to observe carefully all His commandments which I command you today, that the LORD your God will set you high above all nations of the earth. And all these blessings shall come upon you and overtake you, because you obey the voice of the LORD your God:

Blessed shall you be in the city, and blessed shall you be in the country.

Blessed shall be the fruit of your body, the produce of your ground and the increase of your herds, the increase of your cattle and the offspring of your flocks.

Blessed shall be your basket and your kneading bowl.

Blessed shall you be when you come in, and blessed shall you be when you go out.

DEUTERONOMY 28:1–6

Trust in the LORD, and do good;
> Dwell in the land, and feed on His
> > faithfulness.

Delight yourself also in the LORD,
> And He shall give you the desires of
> > your heart.

Commit your way to the LORD,
> Trust also in Him,
> And He shall bring it to pass.

PSALM 37:3–5

"Bring all the tithes into the storehouse,
> That there may be food in My house,
> And try Me now in this,"
> Says the LORD of hosts,
> "If I will not open for you the windows
> > of heaven
> And pour out for you such blessing
> That there will not be room enough to
> > receive it."

MALACHI 3:10

"Do not appear to men to be fasting, but to your Father who is in the secret place; and your Father who sees in secret will reward you openly.

"Do not lay up for yourselves treasures on earth, where moth and rust destroy and where thieves break in and steal; but lay up for yourselves treasures in heaven, where neither moth nor rust destroys and where thieves do not break in and steal. For where your treasure is, there your heart will be also."

MATTHEW 6:18–21

And you shall remember the LORD your God, for it is He who gives you power to get wealth, that He may establish His covenant which He swore to your fathers, as it is this day.

DEUTERONOMY 8:18

BE ACCOUNTABLE TO CHRISTIAN BROTHERS

Two are better than one,
Because they have a good reward for
their labor.
For if they fall, one will lift up his companion.
But woe to him who is alone when
he falls,
For he has no one to help him up.

ECCLESIASTES 4:9–10

Be kindly affectionate to one another with brotherly love, in honor giving preference to one another.

ROMANS 12:10

A man who has friends must himself be
friendly,
But there is a friend who sticks closer
than a brother.

PROVERBS 18:24

As iron sharpens iron,
> So a man sharpens the countenance of
> his friend.

PROVERBS 27:17

Confess your trespasses to one another, and pray for one another, that you may be healed. The effective, fervent prayer of a righteous man avails much.

JAMES 5:16

Since you have purified your souls in obeying the truth through the Spirit in sincere love of the brethren, love one another fervently with a pure heart.

1 PETER 1:22

GOD
LISTENS
TO

FATHERS'

PRAYERS
WHEN . . .

NO ONE ELSE WILL LISTEN

"Ask, and it will be given to you; seek, and you will find; knock, and it will be opened to you. For everyone who asks receives, and he who seeks finds, and to him who knocks it will be opened."

MATTHEW 7:7–8

Rejoice always, pray without ceasing, in everything give thanks; for this is the will of God in Christ Jesus for you.

1 THESSALONIANS 5:16–18

"If My people who are called by My name will humble themselves, and pray and seek My face, and turn from their wicked ways, then I will hear from heaven, and will forgive their sin and heal their land."

2 CHRONICLES 7:14

Therefore take up the whole armor of God, that you may be able to withstand in the evil day, and having done all, to stand.

Ephesians 6:13

Hear me when I call, O God of my
    righteousness!
  You have relieved me in my distress;
  Have mercy on me, and hear my prayer.

Psalm 4:1

Stand therefore, having girded your waist with truth, having put on the breastplate of righteousness, and having shod your feet with the preparation of the gospel of peace; above all, taking the shield of faith with which you will be able to quench all the fiery darts of the wicked one. And take the helmet of salvation, and the sword of the Spirit, which is the word of God; praying always with all prayer and supplication in the Spirit, being watchful to this end with all perseverance and supplication for all the saints.

Ephesians 6:14–18

THEY ASK FOR PATIENCE

For even Christ did not please Himself; but as it is written, "The reproaches of those who reproached You fell on Me." For whatever things were written before were written for our learning, that we through the patience and comfort of the Scriptures might have hope. Now may the God of patience and comfort grant you to be like-minded toward one another, according to Christ Jesus.

ROMANS 15:3–5

Rest in the LORD, and wait patiently for Him;
    Do not fret because of him who prospers
      in his way,
    Because of the man who brings wicked
      schemes to pass.
Cease from anger, and forsake wrath;
    Do not fret—it only causes harm.
For evildoers shall be cut off;
    But those who wait on the LORD,
    They shall inherit the earth.

PSALM 37:7–9

My brethren, count it all joy when you fall into various trials, knowing that the testing of your faith produces patience. But let patience have its perfect work, that you may be perfect and complete, lacking nothing.

JAMES 1:2–4

Therefore we also, since we are surrounded by so great a cloud of witnesses, let us lay aside every weight, and the sin which so easily ensnares us, and let us run with endurance the race that is set before us.

HEBREWS 12:1

Therefore if there is any consolation in Christ, if any comfort of love, if any fellowship of the Spirit, if any affection and mercy, fulfill my joy by being like-minded, having the same love, being of one accord, of one mind. Let nothing be done through selfish ambition or conceit, but in lowliness of mind let each esteem others better than himself. Let each of you look out not only for his own interests, but also for the interests of others.

PHILIPPIANS 2:1–4

THEY ASK FOR GUIDANCE FROM THE HOLY SPIRIT

"And I will pray the Father, and He will give you another Helper, that He may abide with you forever—the Spirit of truth, whom the world cannot receive, because it neither sees Him nor knows Him; but you know Him, for He dwells with you and will be in you."

JOHN 14:16–17

Now the Lord is the Spirit; and where the Spirit of the Lord is, there is liberty. But we all, with unveiled face, beholding as in a mirror the glory of the Lord, are being transformed into the same image from glory to glory, just as by the Spirit of the Lord.

2 CORINTHIANS 3:17–18

Walk in the Spirit, and you shall not fulfill the lust of the flesh. For the flesh lusts against the Spirit, and the Spirit against the flesh; and these are contrary to one another. . . .

Now the works of the flesh are evident, which are: adultery, fornication, uncleanness, lewdness, idolatry, sorcery, hatred, contentions, jealousies, outbursts of wrath, selfish ambitions, dissensions, heresies, envy, murders, drunkenness, revelries, and the like. . . . Those who practice such things will not inherit the kingdom of God.

But the fruit of the Spirit is love, joy, peace, longsuffering, kindness, goodness, faithfulness, gentleness, self-control. Against such there is no law. And those who are Christ's have crucified the flesh with its passions and desires. If we live in the Spirit, let us also walk in the Spirit. Let us not become conceited, provoking one another, envying one another.

GALATIANS 5:16–17, 19–26

THEY CONFESS SINS AND SEEK FORGIVENESS

The Lord is far from the wicked,
>   But He hears the prayer of the righteous.
The light of the eyes rejoices the heart,
>   And a good report makes the bones
>>   healthy.
The ear that hears the rebukes of life
>   Will abide among the wise.
He who disdains instruction despises his
>>   own soul,
>   But he who heeds rebuke gets
>>   understanding.
The fear of the Lord is the instruction of
>>   wisdom,
>   And before honor is humility.

PROVERBS 15:29–33

[Jesus] was the true Light which gives light to every man coming into the world.

JOHN 1:9

"For I will be merciful to their unrighteousness, and their sins and their lawless deeds I will remember no more."

HEBREWS 8:12

To the praise of the glory of His grace, by which He made us accepted in the Beloved.

In Him we have redemption through His blood, the forgiveness of sins, according to the riches of His grace.

EPHESIANS 1:6–7

He who covers his sins will not prosper,
But whoever confesses and forsakes
them will have mercy.

PROVERBS 28:13

RESPONSIBILITIES OVERWHELM THEM

"For the mountains shall depart
   And the hills be removed,
   But My kindness shall not depart from
      you,
   Nor shall My covenant of peace be
      removed,"
   Says the LORD, who has mercy on you.

ISAIAH 54:10

Be strong and of good courage, do not fear nor
be afraid of them; for the LORD your God, He is
the One who goes with you. He will not leave
you nor forsake you.

DEUTERONOMY 31:6

Lift up your eyes on high,
>   And see who has created these things,
>   Who brings out their host by number;
>   He calls them all by name,
>   By the greatness of His might
>   And the strength of His power;
>   Not one is missing.
Why do you say, O Jacob,
>   And speak, O Israel:
>   "My way is hidden from the Lord,
>   And my just claim is passed over by my
>   God"?
Have you not known?
>   Have you not heard?
>   The everlasting God, the Lord,
>   The Creator of the ends of the earth,
>   Neither faints nor is weary.
>   His understanding is unsearchable.
He gives power to the weak,
>   And to those who have no might He
>   increases strength.

Isaiah 40:26–29

"For I know the thoughts that I think toward you, says the Lord, thoughts of peace and not of evil, to give you a future and a hope. Then you will call upon Me and go and pray to Me, and I will listen to you. And you will seek Me and find Me, when you search for Me with all your heart."

JEREMIAH 29:11–13

GOD
FILLS

FATHERS

WITH JOY
WHEN . . .

THEY PRAISE
THE LORD

Praise the LORD!
    Praise God in His sanctuary;
    Praise Him in His mighty firmament!
Praise Him for His mighty acts;
    Praise Him according to His excellent
        greatness!
Praise Him with the sound of the trumpet;
    Praise Him with the lute and harp!
Praise Him with the timbrel and dance;
    Praise Him with stringed instruments
        and flutes!
Praise Him with loud cymbals;
    Praise Him with clashing cymbals!
Let everything that has breath praise the
    LORD.
    Praise the LORD!

PSALM 150:1–6

Know that the LORD, He is God;
> It is He who has made us, and not we
> > ourselves;
> We are His people and the sheep of His
> > pasture.
Enter into His gates with thanksgiving,
> And into His courts with praise.
> Be thankful to Him, and bless His name.
For the LORD is good;
> His mercy is everlasting,
> And His truth endures to all generations.

PSALM 100:3–5

I will extol You, my God, O King;
> And I will bless Your name forever and
> > ever. . . .
Great is the LORD, and greatly to be praised;
> And His greatness is unsearchable.
One generation shall praise Your works to
> > another,
> And shall declare Your mighty acts.

PSALM 145:1, 3–4

I thank You and praise You,
>   O God of my fathers;
>   You have given me wisdom and might,
>   And have now made known to me what
>   we asked of You,
>   For You have made known to us the
>   king's demand.

DANIEL 2:23

May the LORD give you increase more and
>   more,
>   You and your children.
May you be blessed by the LORD,
>   Who made heaven and earth.
The heaven, even the heavens, are the LORD's;
>   But the earth He has given to the
>   children of men.
The dead do not praise the LORD,
>   Nor any who go down into silence.
But we will bless the LORD
>   From this time forth and forevermore.
>   Praise the LORD!

PSALM 115:14–18

THEIR CHILDREN GROW TO LOVE THE LORD

"You are the salt of the earth; but if the salt loses its flavor, how shall it be seasoned? It is then good for nothing but to be thrown out and trampled underfoot by men.

"You are the light of the world. A city that is set on a hill cannot be hidden. Nor do they light a lamp and put it under a basket, but on a lampstand, and it gives light to all who are in the house. Let your light so shine before men, that they may see your good works and glorify your Father in heaven."

MATTHEW 5:13–16

"'And you shall love the LORD your God with all your heart, with all your soul, with all your mind, and with all your strength.' This is the first commandment."

MARK 12:30

[Let] Christ . . . dwell in your hearts through faith; that you, being rooted and grounded in love, may be able to comprehend with all the saints what is the width and length and depth and height—to know the love of Christ which passes knowledge; that you may be filled with all the fullness of God.

EPHESIANS 3:17–19

I love those who love me,
> And those who seek me diligently will
> find me.

PROVERBS 8:17

"As the Father loved Me, I also have loved you; abide in My love. If you keep My commandments, you will abide in My love, just as I have kept My Father's commandments and abide in His love."

JOHN 15:9–10

THEY WORSHIP THE LORD

Give to the Lord the glory due His name;
Bring an offering, and come before Him.
Oh, worship the Lord in the beauty of
holiness!

1 Chronicles 16:29

Let the word of Christ dwell in you richly in all wisdom, teaching and admonishing one another in psalms and hymns and spiritual songs, singing with grace in your hearts to the Lord.

Colossians 3:16

Make a joyful shout to the Lord, all you
lands!
Serve the Lord with gladness;
Come before His presence with singing.

Psalm 100:1–2

Also with the lute I will praise You—
    And Your faithfulness, O my God!
    To You I will sing with the harp,
    O Holy One of Israel.
My lips shall greatly rejoice when I sing
        to You,
    And my soul, which You have redeemed.
My tongue also shall talk of Your
        righteousness all the day long;
    For they are confounded,
    For they are brought to shame
    Who seek my hurt.

PSALM 71:22–24

The LORD lives!
    Blessed be my Rock!
    Let God be exalted,
    The Rock of my salvation!

2 SAMUEL 22:47

GOD
KEEPS

FATHERS

SECURE
WHEN . . .

THEY PUT THE LORD FIRST IN THEIR LIVES

Therefore humble yourselves under the mighty hand of God, that He may exalt you in due time, casting all your care upon Him, for He cares for you.

1 PETER 5:6–7

My son, if you receive my words,
    And treasure my commands within you,
So that you incline your ear to wisdom,
    And apply your heart to understanding;
Yes, if you cry out for discernment,
    And lift up your voice for understanding,
If you seek her as silver,
    And search for her as for hidden
        treasures;
Then you will understand the fear of
    the LORD,
    And find the knowledge of God.

PROVERBS 2:1–5

I will love You, O Lord, my strength.
The Lord is my rock and my fortress and
      my deliverer;
    My God, my strength, in whom I will
      trust;
    My shield and the horn of my salvation,
      my stronghold.
I will call upon the Lord, who is worthy to be
      praised;
    So shall I be saved from my enemies.

PSALM 18:1–3

Therefore submit to God. Resist the devil and he will flee from you. Draw near to God and He will draw near to you. Cleanse your hands, you sinners; and purify your hearts, you double-minded.

JAMES 4:7–8

When wisdom enters your heart,
    And knowledge is pleasant to your soul,
Discretion will preserve you;
    Understanding will keep you,
To deliver you from the way of evil,
    From the man who speaks perverse
      things.

PROVERBS 2:10–12

THEY
CHANGE JOBS

"Therefore I say to you, do not worry about your life, what you will eat or what you will drink; nor about your body, what you will put on. Is not life more than food and the body more than clothing? Look at the birds of the air, for they neither sow nor reap nor gather into barns; yet your heavenly Father feeds them. Are you not of more value than they? . . .

"Therefore do not worry, saying, 'What shall we eat?' or 'What shall we drink?' or 'What shall we wear?' . . . For your heavenly Father knows that you need all these things. But seek first the kingdom of God and His righteousness, and all these things shall be added to you. Therefore do not worry about tomorrow, for tomorrow will worry about its own things. Sufficient for the day is its own trouble."

MATTHEW 6:25–26, 31–34

For no other foundation can anyone lay than that which is laid, which is Jesus Christ. Now if anyone builds on this foundation with gold, silver, precious stones, wood, hay, straw, each one's work will become clear; for the Day will declare it, because it will be revealed by fire; and the fire will test each one's work, of what sort it is. If anyone's work which he has built on it endures, he will receive a reward. If anyone's work is burned, he will suffer loss; but he himself will be saved, yet so as through fire.

1 CORINTHIANS 3:11–15

Do not overwork to be rich;
> Because of your own understanding, cease!
Will you set your eyes on that which is not?
> For riches certainly make themselves wings;
> They fly away like an eagle toward heaven.

PROVERBS 23:4–5

What profit has the worker from that in which he labors? I have seen the God-given task with which the sons of men are to be occupied. He has made everything beautiful in its time. Also He has put eternity in their hearts, except that no one can find out the work that God does from beginning to end.

I know that nothing is better for them than to rejoice, and to do good in their lives, and also that every man should eat and drink and enjoy the good of all his labor—it is the gift of God.

ECCLESIASTES 3:9–13

WORRY AND DOUBT THREATEN THEIR WELL-BEING

The eyes of all look expectantly to You,
And You give them their food in due
season.
You open Your hand
And satisfy the desire of every living thing.
The LORD is righteous in all His ways,
Gracious in all His works.
The LORD is near to all who call upon Him,
To all who call upon Him in truth.
He will fulfill the desire of those who fear Him;
He also will hear their cry and save them.
The LORD preserves all who love Him,
But all the wicked He will destroy.
My mouth shall speak the praise of the LORD,
And all flesh shall bless His holy name
Forever and ever.

PSALM 145:15–21

The work of righteousness will be peace,
>And the effect of righteousness,
>>quietness and assurance forever.

ISAIAH 32:17

You will keep him in perfect peace,
>Whose mind is stayed on You,
>Because he trusts in You.

ISAIAH 26:3

Blessed is every one who fears the LORD,
>Who walks in His ways. . . .
The LORD bless you out of Zion,
>And may you see the good of Jerusalem
>All the days of your life.
Yes, may you see your children's children.
>Peace be upon Israel!

PSALM 128:1, 5–6

Blessed be the LORD,
>Who daily loads us with benefits,
>The God of our salvation! *Selah*.

PSALM 68:19

THEIR FAMILIES FACE ENEMIES

Be strong and of good courage, do not fear nor be afraid of them; for the LORD your God, He is the One who goes with you. He will not leave you nor forsake you.

DEUTERONOMY 31:6

"But if you indeed obey His voice and do all that I speak, then I will be an enemy to your enemies and an adversary to your adversaries."

EXODUS 23:22

The eternal God is your refuge,
  And underneath are the everlasting
      arms;
  He will thrust out the enemy from before
      you,
  And will say, "Destroy!"

DEUTERONOMY 33:27

Arise, O Lord!

O God, lift up Your hand!

Do not forget the humble.

Why do the wicked renounce God?

He has said in his heart,

"You will not require an account."

But You have seen, for You observe trouble
and grief,

To repay it by Your hand.

The helpless commits himself to You;

You are the helper of the fatherless.

Break the arm of the wicked and the
evil man;

Seek out his wickedness until You find
none.

The Lord is King forever and ever;

The nations have perished out of His land.

Lord, You have heard the desire of the
humble;

You will prepare their heart;

You will cause Your ear to hear,

To do justice to the fatherless and the
oppressed,

That the man of the earth may oppress
no more.

PSALM 10:12–18

GOD
COMFORTS

FATHERS

WHEN . . .

THEIR LOVED ONES ARE ILL

Is anyone among you sick? Let him call for the elders of the church, and let them pray over him, anointing him with oil in the name of the Lord. And the prayer of faith will save the sick, and the Lord will raise him up. And if he has committed sins, he will be forgiven. Confess your trespasses to one another, and pray for one another, that you may be healed. The effective, fervent prayer of a righteous man avails much.

JAMES 5:14–16

Heal me, O LORD, and I shall be healed;
　　Save me, and I shall be saved,
　　For You are my praise.

JEREMIAH 17:14

"If you diligently heed the voice of the LORD your God and do what is right in His sight, give ear to His commandments and keep all His statutes, I will put none of the diseases on you which I have brought on the Egyptians. For I am the LORD who heals you."

EXODUS 15:26

My son, give attention to my words;
    Incline your ear to my sayings.
Do not let them depart from your eyes;
    Keep them in the midst of your heart;
For they are life to those who find them,
    And health to all their flesh.

PROVERBS 4:20–22

Jesus said to him, "If you can believe, all things are possible to him who believes."

Immediately the father of the child cried out and said with tears, "Lord, I believe; help my unbelief!"

MARK 9:23–24

THEIR LOVED ONES DON'T UNDERSTAND THEM

Let love be without hypocrisy. Abhor what is evil. Cling to what is good. Be kindly affectionate to one another with brotherly love, in honor giving preference to one another.

ROMANS 12:9–10

"For if you love those who love you, what reward have you? Do not even the tax collectors do the same? And if you greet your brethren only, what do you do more than others? Do not even the tax collectors do so? Therefore you shall be perfect, just as your Father in heaven is perfect."

MATTHEW 5:46–48

Husbands, likewise, dwell with them with understanding, giving honor to the wife, as to the weaker vessel, and as being heirs together of the grace of life, that your prayers may not be hindered.

Finally, all of you be of one mind, having compassion for one another; love as brothers, be tenderhearted, be courteous; not returning evil for evil or reviling for reviling, but on the contrary blessing, knowing that you were called to this, that you may inherit a blessing. For

> "He who would love life
> And see good days,
> Let him refrain his tongue from evil,
> And his lips from speaking deceit.
> Let him turn away from evil and do
> good;
> Let him seek peace and pursue it."

1 PETER 3:7–11

THEY MUST DISCIPLINE THEIR LOVED ONES

My son, do not despise the chastening of the
　　Lord,
　　Nor detest His correction;
　　For whom the Lord loves He corrects,
　　Just as a father the son in whom he
　　　　delights.

PROVERBS 3:11–12

We have had human fathers who corrected us,
and we paid them respect. Shall we not much
more readily be in subjection to the Father of
spirits and live? For they indeed for a few days
chastened us as seemed best to them, but He
for our profit, that we may be partakers of His
holiness. Now no chastening seems to be joyful for the present, but painful; nevertheless,
afterward it yields the peaceable fruit of righteousness to those who have been trained by it.

HEBREWS 12:9–11

Therefore be very courageous to keep and to do all that is written in the Book of the Law of Moses, lest you turn aside from it to the right hand or to the left. . . . But you shall hold fast to the Lord your God, as you have done to this day.

JOSHUA 23:6, 8

My son, keep my words,
    And treasure my commands within you.
Keep my commands and live,
    And my law as the apple of your eye.
Bind them on your fingers;
        Write them on the tablet of your heart.

PROVERBS 7:1–3

Whoever loves instruction loves knowledge,
    But he who hates correction is stupid.
A good man obtains favor from the LORD,
    But a man of wicked intentions He will
        condemn.
A man is not established by wickedness,
    But the root of the righteous cannot be
        moved.

PROVERBS 12:1–3

GOD'S
SPECIAL
LOVE IS
WITH

FATHERS

WHEN . . .

THEY BRING THEIR PROBLEMS TO HIM

"For the eyes of the LORD are on the
     righteous,
And His ears are open to their prayers;
But the face of the LORD is against those
     who do evil."

And who is he who will harm you if you
become followers of what is good? But even
if you should suffer for righteousness' sake,
you are blessed. "And do not be afraid of their
threats, nor be troubled." But sanctify the Lord
God in your hearts, and always be ready to give
a defense to everyone who asks you a reason for
the hope that is in you, with meekness and fear.

1 PETER 3:12–15

But Jesus looked at them and said to them,
"With men this is impossible, but with God all
things are possible."

MATTHEW 19:26

Yes, we had the sentence of death in ourselves, that we should not trust in ourselves but in God who raises the dead, who delivered us from so great a death, and does deliver us; in whom we trust that He will still deliver us.

2 CORINTHIANS 1:9–10

Now thanks be to God who always leads us in triumph in Christ, and through us diffuses the fragrance of His knowledge in every place. For we are to God the fragrance of Christ among those who are being saved and among those who are perishing. To the one we are the aroma of death leading to death, and to the other the aroma of life leading to life. And who is sufficient for these things? For we are not, as so many, peddling the word of God; but as of sincerity, but as from God, we speak in the sight of God in Christ.

2 CORINTHIANS 2:14–17

GOD'S SPECIAL LOVE IS WITH FATHERS
WHEN . . .

THEY RELY ON HIM TO GUIDE THEIR CHILDREN

When you roam, they will lead you;
    When you sleep, they will keep you;
    And when you awake, they will speak
        with you.
For the commandment is a lamp,
    And the law a light;
    Reproofs of instruction are the way of life.

PROVERBS 6:22–23

"I will go before you
    And make the crooked places straight;
    I will break in pieces the gates of bronze
    And cut the bars of iron.
I will give you the treasures of darkness
    And hidden riches of secret places,
    That you may know that I, the LORD,
    Who call you by your name,
    Am the God of Israel."

ISAIAH 45:2–3

Have you not known?
>   Have you not heard?
>   The everlasting God, the LORD,
>   The Creator of the ends of the earth,
>   Neither faints nor is weary.
>   His understanding is unsearchable.
He gives power to the weak,
>   And to those who have no might He
>   increases strength.
Even the youths shall faint and be weary,
>   And the young men shall utterly fall,
But those who wait on the LORD
>   Shall renew their strength;
>   They shall mount up with wings like
>   eagles,
>   They shall run and not be weary,
>   They shall walk and not faint.

ISAIAH 40:28–31

"Fear not, for I am with you;
>   Be not dismayed, for I am your God.
>   I will strengthen you,
>   Yes, I will help you,
>   I will uphold you with My righteous right
>   hand."

ISAIAH 41:10

"I, the LORD, have called You in righteousness,
   And will hold Your hand;
   I will keep You and give You as a
      covenant to the people,
   As a light to the Gentiles."

ISAIAH 42:6

GOD'S SPECIAL LOVE IS WITH FATHERS
WHEN . . .

THEY FORGIVE
THEIR CHILDREN

He made known His ways to Moses,
> His acts to the children of Israel.

The LORD is merciful and gracious,
> Slow to anger, and abounding in mercy.

He will not always strive with us,
> Nor will He keep His anger forever.

He has not dealt with us according to
> our sins,
> Nor punished us according to our
> iniquities.

For as the heavens are high above the earth,
> So great is His mercy toward those who
> fear Him;

As far as the east is from the west,
> So far has He removed our
> transgressions from us.

As a father pities his children,
> So the LORD pities those who fear Him.

PSALM 103:7–13

"Take heed to yourselves. If your brother sins against you, rebuke him; and if he repents, forgive him. And if he sins against you seven times in a day, and seven times in a day returns to you, saying, 'I repent,' you shall forgive him."

LUKE 17:3–4

Then Peter came to Him and said, "Lord, how often shall my brother sin against me, and I forgive him? Up to seven times?"

Jesus said to him, "I do not say to you, up to seven times, but up to seventy times seven."

MATTHEW 18:21–22

"For if you forgive men their trespasses, your heavenly Father will also forgive you. But if you do not forgive men their trespasses, neither will your Father forgive your trespasses."

MATTHEW 6:14–15

THEY TRUST GOD AND WAIT FOR HIS ANSWERS

"I am the Lord, and there is no other;
    There is no God besides Me.
    I will gird you, though you have not
        known Me,
That they may know from the rising of the
        sun to its setting
    That there is none besides Me.
    I am the Lord, and there is no other."

ISAIAH 45:5–6

Do not be deceived, my beloved brethren. Every good gift and every perfect gift is from above, and comes down from the Father of lights, with whom there is no variation or shadow of turning.

JAMES 1:16–17

My soul, wait silently for God alone,
For my expectation is from Him.
He only is my rock and my salvation;
He is my defense;
I shall not be moved.
In God is my salvation and my glory;
The rock of my strength,
And my refuge, is in God.
Trust in Him at all times, you people;
Pour out your heart before Him;
God is a refuge for us. *Selah*.

PSALM 62:5–8

Every word of God is pure;
He is a shield to those who put their trust
in Him.

PROVERBS 30:5

The LORD your God in your midst,
The Mighty One, will save;
He will rejoice over you with gladness,
He will quiet you with His love,
He will rejoice over you with singing.

ZEPHANIAH 3:17

NOTES

NOTES

NOTES

NOTES

NOTES

NOTES